CONTENTS

Some words are shown in bold, **like this**.
You can find out what they mean by looking in the glossary.

WHAT WAS EGYPTIAN ART?

Ancient Egypt was full of dazzling colours. Under the blue sky was the silver River Nile, the red, orange, and brown earth, golden sands and green grass. Ancient Egyptian art reflects these colourful surroundings. By studying the art, we can discover how the people lived, worked, and what they believed in. Most of the Egyptian art that has survived is to do with their religious beliefs. Much of it, such as tomb paintings, mummy cases, models, and statues, are related to their dead. The ancient Egyptians believed that people came back to life after they had died.

Winnowing corn, part of a wall painting from the tomb of Nakht, c. 1320 BC

This wall painting comes from the tomb of the royal **scribe**, Nahkt. It tells us about his life. Here, his servants are separating (winnowing) corn. The **composition** of the painting is well balanced. Egyptian paintings are like colourful diagrams.

Ancient Egyptian Art

Susie Hodge

www.heinemann.co.uk/library
Visit our website to find out more information about Heinemann Library books.

To order:
☎ Phone 44 (0) 1865 888112
📄 Send a fax to 44 (0) 1865 314091
💻 Visit the Heinemann bookshop at www.heinemann.co.uk/library to browse our catalogue and order online.

First published in Great Britain by Heinemann Library, Halley Court, Jordan Hill, Oxford OX2 8EJ, part of Harcourt Education.

Heinemann is a registered trademark of Harcourt Education Ltd.

Editorial: Clare Lewis
Design: Victoria Bevan, Michelle Lisseter, and Q2A Media
Illustrations: Oxford Illustrators
Picture Research: Erica Newbery
Production: Helen McCreath

Printed in China

ISBN 978 0 431 05669 2 (hardback)
10 09 08 07 06
10 9 8 7 6 5 4 3 2 1

ISBN 978 0 431 05801 6 (paperback)
11 10 09 08 07
10 9 8 7 6 5 4 3 2 1

British Library Cataloguing in Publication Data
Hodge, Susie
Art in History: Ancient Egyptian Art – 2nd edition
709.3'2
A full catalogue record for this book is available from the British Library.

Acknowledgements
The publishers would like to thank the following for permission to reproduce photographs:
AKG Images / Erich Lessing p.9; Ancient Art & Architecture Collection pp.4, 6, 18, 19; Bridgeman Art Library / Giraudon p.13; British Museum pp.5, 7, 14–15, 17, 21, 24, 28–9; C M Dixon pp.10, 20; Colorific! M Brooke p.27; Corbis: R Wood p.11, M Nicholson p.25, C & J Lenars p.26; Werner Forman Archive: British Museum p.12, Egyptian Museum, Cairo pp.16, 22–3.

Cover picture of a banquet scene from the tomb of Nebumun, reproduced with permission of Werner Forman/Werner Forman Archive/British Museum, London.

Every effort has been made to contact copyright holders of any material reproduced in this book. Any omissions will be rectified in subsequent printings if notice is given to the publishers.

The paper used to print this book comes from sustainable resources.

Rules of art

The layout of all art was important. Nothing was left to chance. Everything was measured and put in its place for a purpose. All art – statues, paintings, and buildings – obeyed rules of balance and proportion. Every artist had to learn the rules. For example, statues of seated people had to have their hands on their knees. Men statues had to have darker skin than women statues. Gods had special features and were often shown with the heads of particular animals.

Three kingdoms

Ancient Egyptian history is divided into three main periods: the Old Kingdom (about 2686– 2181 BC), Middle Kingdom (about 2040–1782 BC), and New Kingdom (about 1570–1070 BC). The wall painting on page 4 was painted during the Middle Kingdom. Art did not change much over 3,000 years, but there were some differences between the art of each period.

Little pictures

Artists also had to learn to write. The early form of Egyptian writing was made up of tiny pictures. Even writing was an art form in ancient Egypt.

Katep and his wife Hetepheres, from Giza, c. 2300 BC, height 47.5cm (19in), **limestone**

This statue was made during the Old Kingdom. It follows the rules of art. The figures' hands are on their knees. The wife's skin is pale yellow while her husband's is red. Facial details were always painted in black.

MATERIALS AND METHODS

Egyptian boys usually followed the same trade as their parents. Women and girls were not expected to have a trade; they cared for the home. But if a craftsman had no sons, he could teach his trade to his daughters. All artists were seen as craftsmen. They trained from as young as five years old in workshops alongside other craftsmen, such as sculptors and jewellers.

One man, who was like a chief designer, supervised them all. He planned their work and checked that the standards were high. Most of the work followed a traditional pattern. Occasionally a fresh design was demanded, for example when a new pharaoh (king) came to the throne.

Paintings give information. This shows us jewellers in the craftsmen's workshop. The artists who painted this had a good sense of design and colour. Although it seems a simple picture, it is well balanced and includes plenty of detail. What do you think the jewellers are doing?

Jewellers at work, part of a wall-painting from the tomb of Nebamun at Thebes, c. 1400 BC

Egyptian artists did not sign their art because they worked in teams. If an artist was particularly skilful at copying past work and handling materials, he might be given more work. But usually only the supervisor, or chief designer, became well known.

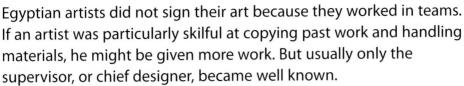

Preparing paints, brushes, and surfaces

Brushes of different sizes were made from lengths of coarse palm leaves or knotted rope that had been beaten at one end, so that they looked a bit like stiff shaving brushes. Paint was made from finely ground **minerals** mixed with **vegetable gum** or egg. It gave a smooth finish. This kind of paint is called **tempera**. If a stone or wood surface was too rough to paint on, it was coated with a layer of chalky liquid that dried to make a hard, smooth surface. Compositions were drawn with the help of a grid, marked out in red, to make sure that everything was of the right proportion.

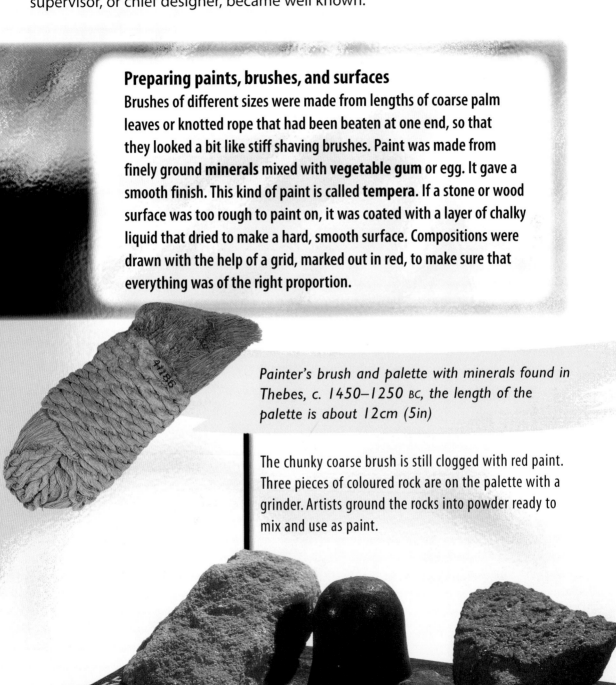

Painter's brush and palette with minerals found in Thebes, c. 1450–1250 BC, the length of the palette is about 12cm (5in)

The chunky coarse brush is still clogged with red paint. Three pieces of coloured rock are on the palette with a grinder. Artists ground the rocks into powder ready to mix and use as paint.

ART AND THE AFTERLIFE

The ancient Egyptians believed that when a person died, their spirit left their body, but came back later and lived an afterlife. This meant that the body had to be preserved so that the returning spirit could use it. And, the person had to be buried with all the items they might need in the afterlife.

Preserving the body

The Egyptians preserved the body by **embalming** it. Firstly, they removed internal organs which would cause the body to rot.

These were stored in containers called canopic jars. Then they dried out the body by soaking it in a salty liquid for about 40 days. Next, they wrapped the body in bandages to make a mummy. The mummy was put into a mummy-shaped coffin (sarcophagus). The richer people had more care taken over them. Important people had more than one sarcophagus, which they stacked inside each other.

Painting on Djedbastinfanth's wooden coffin, at El Hiba, after 600 BC

These scenes show bodies being prepared for burial. The painting is like a diagram. Each section shows different stages in the process. The objects with animal heads, above the mummy, are canopic jars. The colours would have been much brighter when it was first painted.

Art for the afterlife

People were buried with items they would need for the afterlife, such as food, furniture, and clothing. They also included models of houses, boats, servants, and animals, which would change from models to the real thing in the afterlife. Again, the more important people had extra items buried with them. The craftsmen who made the models could produce simple clay models, or complicated and magnificently painted models, depending on how much they were paid!

These are small models of servants. They would have been buried with their mistress or master so that they could serve him or her in the afterlife.

9

SIGNS AND SYMBOLS

About 5,000 years ago Egyptian scribes began drawing simple pictures to represent objects and sounds. This was one of the first forms of writing. They wrote on **papyrus scrolls** with coloured inks and pens made from the softened ends of reeds.

Egyptian writing

Gradually words were built up out of several different signs. To clarify the meaning of a word, a picture of the object or action was sometimes added at the end. This picture writing, called **hieroglyphics**, was used for religious writings and for **inscriptions** on monuments. There were about 750 different hieroglyphs. Most are pictures of people, animals, plants, or objects. It took about 12 years to learn to write in the Egyptian script. Many artists and scribes (one person often did both jobs) started learning at the age of four!

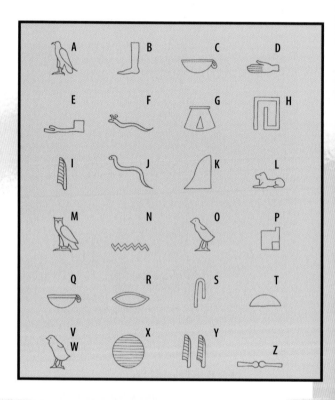

From the papyrus of Hunefer, at Thebes, c. 1320 BC, height 40cm (16in)

The scene of priests and mourners at the entrance to Hunefer's tomb shows burial rituals in signs and **symbols**. The jackal-headed priest supports the mummy as Hunefer's wife, Nesha, and another woman mourn him. Behind stands the priest in charge, wearing a leopard skin. The priests, painted in different shades of brown, make offerings.

Relief, from the tomb of Queen Nefertari, about 1250 BC, limestone

The colours in this relief are still bright, having been preserved by the dry climate. Queen Nefertari was the wife of a great king, Rameses II. The hieroglyphs mean: "Words spoken by the Osirified Great Royal Wife Nefertari, beloved of Mut". (Osirified means dead and now a goddess; Mut was the wife of the god Amun-Re, king of the gods.)

Make a mummy and message

Materials:
- card
- paper
- scissors
- felt-tipped pens
- paints
- glue

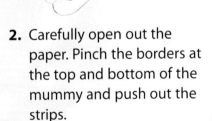

1. Fold a piece of paper in half lengthways. Along the fold draw and cut out the shape of half a mummy. Make cuts side-by-side from the folded edge, out to the mummy outline, leaving an uncut border of 2cm (1in) width. Gently bend the cut strips backwards and forwards.

2. Carefully open out the paper. Pinch the borders at the top and bottom of the mummy and push out the strips.

3. Paint around the mummy. Fold a sheet of card in half lengthways and glue the mummy on to it. Write your own hieroglyphic message on the card.

PAINTING TECHNIQUES

The most important Egyptian paintings were on the walls of temples, tombs, and palaces. But the Egyptians also painted on papyrus.

Plans and grids

Wall paintings were made to a strict plan. First, plaster was smoothed over uneven walls. Then, an outline artist would mark it with a grid of squares, using string soaked in paint. A trainee artist would draw in the scene, copying from a picture on papyrus. Lastly, painters would fill in the outlines with bright colours.

This wall painting gives plenty of information about fish, birds, plants, and also hunting methods.

Wall painting from the tomb of Nebanum, Thebes, c. 1400 BC, height 95cm (38in)

This painting shows Sennedjem and his wife ploughing, harvesting, and praying in the next world. The Egyptians showed objects as being near or far away by painting the people in front in the lowest row and the people farthest away in the highest row.

Flat pictures

People look flat and strange in Egyptian paintings because they were painted in a particular way. Important people were painted larger than others. Heads were shown from the side, because this was clearer than a face-on view. Eyes and the top half of the body were shown from the front, but arms and legs were shown from the side, so that they were easier to see. A foot was always shown from the inner side. Men were painted a reddish-brown colour, while women were pale yellow.

The artists did not really think that people looked like this – they were following rules. Their paintings had messages in them, instead of being lifelike portraits. Egyptian artists followed these rules for nearly 3,000 years.

Paint palette

Brightly coloured paints used by the Egyptians were made from ground minerals. Yellow, red, and brown came from earth; white came from crushed limestone; green was a mixture of blue powdered copper and yellow earth; black came from soot; and blue came from a stone called **lapis lazuli**. Sometimes gold dust was used as paint, too.

ART FOR THE GODS

Gods and goddesses were important to all Egyptians. They controlled life, death, and the natural world. Wall paintings in the tomb of Tuthmosis III show 700 Egyptian gods. The most important were Ra, the sun god, and Osiris, the god of the afterlife.

Palaces of the gods

A temple was the palace of a god. The ruling pharaoh would order a temple to be built for a particular god or goddess. A statue of the god was made for its spirit to live in. Only the high priests could see the statue for fear of insulting the god, so it had to be hidden in a shrine. Priests would offer this statue perfumes, clothing, and food. Ordinary people also came with offerings.

Artists and craftsmen were always needed to make art for the gods. They built and decorated temple and tomb walls. They also made statues of the gods and goddesses and painted stories about them on papyrus. Artists and craftsmen often worked deep in the darkness of tombs and temples. Their only light was from candle-type lamps or from bronze mirrors that reflected sunlight into the tomb.

Animal features

As you can see, the Egyptians believed that gods and goddesses could take on the form of a particular bird or animal. Some had the body of a human and the head of an animal or bird, such as Anubis the jackal, and Horus the falcon. Every artist had to know what each god and goddess looked like.

The Book of the Dead was a book that was buried in tombs with the dead. This painting shows the jackal-headed god Anubis leading Hunefer to the scales where his heart will be weighed against a feather from the goddess of truth. If the heart is lighter than the feather, then he passes the test and is led to Osiris.

The Judgement of Hunefer from the Book of the Dead, c. 1320 BC

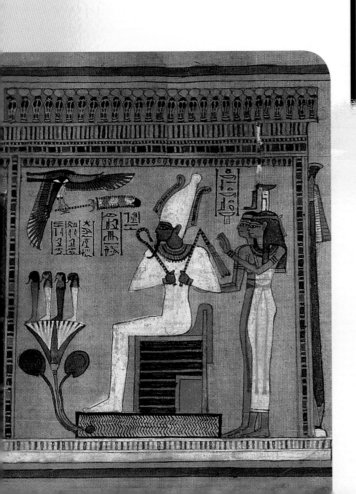

ART FOR THE KING

As we have seen, the Egyptians believed in many gods. These gods affected different parts of people's lives. The pharaoh, king of Egypt, was also seen as a god. He was not as important as some of the other gods, but he was not just a human either. Because of this, pharaohs had to be obeyed, even if people did not want to do as a pharaoh ordered. The pharaoh Amenhotep IV (1350–34 BC) changed people's beliefs and artistic practices for at least as long as he lived.

A different belief

Amenhotep IV believed in worshipping just one god, the sun god called Aten. He changed his name to Akhenaten in honour of this god. He built a new capital city, Akhetaten, and moved there. We are not sure if he told people that they were not allowed to worship the other gods that he had rejected. But we do know that many people followed Amenhotep's beliefs because he was their pharaoh.

King Akhenaten and Queen Nefertiti are sitting on stools, relaxing with their daughters. The sun god, Aten, shines down on them all. Kings had never been shown in natural poses like this before.

King Akhenaten with his wife and three of their daughters, from Amarna, c. 1350 BC, 33 x 39cm (13 x 15in), limestone relief

A different art

Akhenaten believed that art ought to be more lifelike. He encouraged artists to forget the rules of painting and show things as they really are. Again, we do not know if he forced artists to change their ways, but if anyone wanted to work for him they would have to work the way he wished. As soon as Akhenaten died, artists went back to the old rules.

Look at the musicians as they entertain guests at a meal. Compare their faces, bodies, hands and feet.

Wall painting from the tomb of Nebamun at western Thebes, c. 1356 BC, height 61cm (24in)

A closer look

Look closer at the relief opposite. Akhenaten's daughters may seem unnatural and rather like tiny adults instead of small children, but they are pictured almost front-facing. Now look at Akhenaten's feet – you can see his toes! This shows an interest in making the images look three dimensional, instead of flat like the set forms of traditional Egyptian art.

RELIEF ART

Egyptian paintings were smooth and flat, but artists also made raised pictures called **reliefs**. Sculptors carved the reliefs. During the Old and Middle Kingdoms they were usually in soft limestone. In the New Kingdom they were often in **sandstone.**

The schoolroom, from the tomb of Horemheb, c. 1300 BC, relief

This relief shows pupils working in a schoolroom. The realistic relief shows children sitting in rows and writing at wooden desks. The pupils are shown in a realistic style. Egyptians liked to show everyday scenes like this in their art.

Many bold reliefs like this were found in the tomb of Ptah-hotep, an important man who worked for the king. The figures, although set in the usual Egyptian style, appear to move along as they carry their offerings of lotus flowers, livestock, and food.

Servants bringing offerings to Ptah-hotep, Saqqara, c. 2450 BC, limestone, height of each figure, 42cm (17in)

Coloured carvings

Granite, alabaster, limestone, sandstone, and richly coloured rocks were hacked out of **quarries** near the River Nile to be used for building and carving. Next to the reliefs, sculptors also carved detailed and precise inscriptions, and images of gods and pharaohs. Any mistakes were filled in with plaster.

There were two kinds of relief. Raised relief had the main subjects standing out from the background. Sunken reliefs had the main subjects cut into the surface, with the background standing out. Sunken reliefs are usually on outside walls where there is strong sunlight, or on monuments and pillars.

Reliefs show every kind of activity, from farming to feasting, from jewellery-making to dancing. Some of the scenes follow a sequence, showing how a task or activity was done, and some have a message.

How relief artists worked

Relief artists worked in the same way as painters. First they dipped a string in red paint and stretched it across the stone vertically and horizontally to make a grid. Then they carefully drew in the outline. Once the drawing had been finished and had been approved by the supervisor, specialist stonecutters took over. After the picture had been carved, artists painted it with brilliant colours to make it stand out even more.

SECRETS OF SCULPTURE

Making statues

Sculptors worked close to the quarries. With the help of the **masons**, they found a suitable block of stone. Other artists marked the stone with a grid and copied the outline of the statue from the sculptor's drawing in red or black ink.

Using simple **chisels** and **mallets**, they chipped all around the stone until the right shape appeared.

The statue was tied to a sledge and dragged to the River Nile. The ground was sprinkled with water to help it slide. It was put on a boat and carried to the temple or tomb it was made for. This only happened during a flood tide, when the river was at its highest. People would line the route to worship the statue as it passed.

When it reached its destination, workers polished it with sand, water, and stones that were covered with leather. Lastly, they painted it.

This bust of Queen Nefertiti, wife of Akhenaten, was found among the remains of a sculptor's studio in Tell el-Amarna. Her eyes are made from rock crystals. The statue follows the style of the more lifelike art of Akhenaten's reign.

Nefertiti, c. 1360BC, height 50cm (20in), painted limestone

Making models

Sculptors used ivory, wood, and metal as well as stone. They carved small wooden models of people doing everyday tasks to accompany a dead person on his journey to the next world. One Egyptian word for sculptor means "he who keeps alive".

Bronze statuettes of gods and goddesses were also made for tombs. First a model was made in beeswax and coated with clay, leaving a small hole in the base. The model was then heated to harden the clay and melt the wax, which then poured out through the hole. Next, molten bronze was poured in. When the bronze had cooled and hardened, the clay was broken, leaving the bronze model.

This kneeling bronze statuette, from the New Kingdom, is holding two offering pots. The king's name is on the **cartouches** on his shoulder. The figure would have been placed in a tomb in front of a larger figure of a god or goddess.

King Pimay, 770 BC, height 25.5cm (10in), bronze

EGYPTIAN STATUES

Most statues were of gods and goddesses, pharaohs, and queens. Sculptors were skilled at carving both small and gigantic statues.

The Great Sphinx at Giza, c. 2550 BC, 73 x 20m (240 x 67 ft), sandstone

Built in the Old Kingdom, this giant statue guards the great **pyramids** at Giza. Sculptors used scaffolding to carve the hunk of rock found in a local quarry. It has the body of a lion and head of a human, and is thought to represent King Khafre. It is the largest free-standing sculpture that survives from the ancient world.

Statue stories

It is said that a young prince once rested against the head of the Great Sphinx when its body was covered in sand. The sun god appeared and promised to make him king if he freed the Sphinx from the sand. The prince did so, and became Tuthmosis IV.
The largest known statue ever to be cut from a single block of granite stood in the temple of a king known as Rameses the Great. Fragments of an even larger Egyptian statue have been found, including a big toe that is the size of a person.

Symbols of life

Statues, like paintings and reliefs, were not meant to copy nature. They were meant to be symbols. Sculptors worked to strict rules. Statues were always youthful figures. Men stood with the left foot forward, arms by sides or seated on a throne. Women stood or sat rigidly. Most statues were painted, symbolizing the colourfulness of the world.

Tutankhamen's tomb

The tomb of a particularly rich Egyptian pharaoh was discovered in the 1920s. It was that of Tutankhamen (King Akhenaten's younger brother). Tutankhamen became pharaoh after Akhenaten. He died when he was 18. In his tomb were priceless treasures, including jewellery, weapons, and furniture covered with gold and decorations of semi-precious stones.

The mask of Tutankhamen, from a tomb in the Valley of the Kings, c. 1330 BC, height 54cm (21in), gold, glass, and semi-precious stones

This mask, made from 110 kg (242 lbs) of gold, covered the face of Tutankhamen's mummy. On the forehead are the vulture-goddess of Upper Egypt and the serpent-goddess of Lower Egypt. All pharaohs used these symbols to show that they ruled both parts of Egypt. All pharaohs also wore a false "beard" for ceremonies.

23

EGYPTIAN BUILDINGS

Like Egyptian paintings, buildings were of geometric design. Temples were built of stone so they would last for ever. Houses and palaces were made of mud bricks, mixed with grit and straw, shaped, and hardened in the sun.

Brilliant colours

Palaces and rich people's houses had high windows to let in the air and light, but to keep the inside cool. Walls, floors, and ceilings were coated in plaster, then painted white or tiled in brilliant colours. Some walls had **murals** painted on them. Gardens with pools surrounded some houses, but most people relaxed on the flat roofs.

The royal **scribe**, Nakht, and his wife, Tjiui, stand in front of their typically Egyptian house.

Detail from the Book of the Dead, *about 1320 BC, paint on papyrus*

Furniture for the wealthy

Only rich Egyptians could furnish their houses with chairs, beds, chests, and tables, which were probably carved from local fig wood. Chairs were a sign of wealth. They also had painted wall-hangings. The pharaoh and nobles had furniture made of costly ebony or cedar wood, inlaid with gold or precious stones.

Homes for the gods

The ruling pharaoh ordered temples to be built in honour of gods or goddesses. **Architects** designed them, drawing plans and making small models first for the pharaoh to approve.

The forecourt of the temple of the god Amun-Re, at Karnak, 2000–1000 BC, sandstone, limestone, and granite

Every Egyptian temple had a sacred lake. This temple was huge. The statue is 15 metres (49 feet) high.

An amazing temple

During the New Kingdom, Rameses II ordered an amazing temple to be built. Stonecutters hollowed it out of the **sandstone** cliff, leaving pillars in place as ceiling supports. Sculptors carved eight pillars into 10-metre (33-foot) tall statues of Rameses, and four giant seated figures of him guarding the temple entrance.

Painters then added colours and decorated the walls with hieroglyphs and reliefs. They always followed the strict rules of temple decoration. Twice a year, on Rameses' birthday and the anniversary of his coronation, the rising sun reached the innermost part of the temple, lighting up the statues of Rameses and the god Amun.

THE POWERFUL PYRAMIDS

Pharaohs' tombs

The most famous Egyptian buildings are the pyramids, which were built as tombs for pharaohs. Pyramids were not built all through the ancient Egyptian period (which lasted from about 3000 BC to 30 BC). Pharaohs were also buried in other sorts of tombs.

Pyramid building only went on from about 2700 BC to 2400 BC, during the Old Kingdom. These pyramids are famous for several reasons. Firstly, they are some of the few remaining ancient Egyptian structures. Secondly, they were magnificently decorated. We get much of our information about ancient Egypt from the painting and carvings in the pyramids. Thirdly, they raise a lot of questions that we can only guess the answers to.

The most famous and largest of all pyramids is the Great Pyramid of King Khufu, or Cheops. It was once coated with gleaming white limestone and the top capped with shining gold. It is one of the Seven Wonders of the ancient world.

The Great Pyramid at Giza, c. 2660 BC, height 162m (531ft), sandstone

Stairways to heaven

No one really knows why the Egyptians buried their kings in tombs of this shape. The first pyramid to be built was not smooth-sided, but built with giant steps. Some people believe they represented giant steps to heaven. Most later pyramids were made with smooth sides. No one really knows exactly how they were built, either.

The largest pyramid of all contains 2 million blocks of stone, each weighing about the same as a double-decker bus. Each block was moved without any machinery. All they had were wooden rollers, ropes, and pulleys, and bronze tools to cut with. Yet all the blocks fit together so closely that you cannot fit a piece of paper between any of them. They must have taken a lot of people many years to build.

Step Pyramid of King Djoser at Saqqara, c. 2630 BC, height 65m (213ft), sandstone

This is one of the oldest stone structures in Egypt. It was designed by Imhotep, a royal **architect** and high priest of the sun god.

Seeing in the dark

It is remarkable that Egyptian art is so exact, colourful, and skilful, when most of it was made in the gloomy darkness of tombs.

THE BEGINNINGS OF MODERN DESIGN

Ancient Egyptian art was so balanced, carefully worked out, and organized that it has a power which can still be seen today. The artists were mostly **anonymous**, producing work mainly for religious purposes, not decoration. They could not express themselves freely like artists can today. They had to be exact, showing nature in a set way. They could never ignore the rules.

Painted in the New Kingdom, this shows nature in the clearest way. Like a map, the pond is flat-looking, shown from above so that you can see the fish, birds, and plants. Trees, though, are clearer when seen from the side.

A wall-painting from a tomb in Thebes, about 1400 BC, 64cm (25 in)

Art Deco

In 1922, when the tomb of Tutankhamen was discovered, there was a new interest in Egyptian art. Designers who were already developing a new style called Art Deco began adding Egyptian-looking touches to their designs. This suited the style well. Like ancient Egyptian art, Art Deco could be applied to all art, from paintings and sculpture, to furniture and buildings. Designers put bright colours with the **geometric** shapes, but used modern materials.

Graphic design

Hieroglyphics have also been a great influence on **graphic design**. Look out for signs and symbols that could be modern hieroglyphs, like road signs and washing instructions.

New or old? Is this a modern design, or was it painted about 4,000 years ago?

It is in fact a detail from the inside of the wooden coffin of a doctor Seni. It was made in about 2000 BC. Artists have been learning from balanced compositions like this for over 4,000 years.

Art forever

Ancient Egyptian art was made for eternity. In a way, artists achieved that. Their work has lasted and influenced others for centuries. The ancient Greeks and Romans copied their **techniques** and ways of showing nature for years. Scribes in the Middle Ages copied their illustrated papyrus designs, to make beautiful **illuminated manuscripts**. In the early 1900s, a style of art and design called Art Deco used some of the ancient Egyptians' flat, geometric compositions.

TIMELINE

FIND OUT MORE

You can find out more about Egyptian art in books and on the Internet. Use a search engine such as www.yahooligans.com to search for information. A search for the words "Ancient Egyptian art" will bring back lots of results, but it may be difficult to find the information you want. Try refining your search to look for some of the ideas mentioned in this book, such as "relief art".

More books to read

Gaff, Jackie. *Excavating the Past: Ancient Egypt*. Oxford: Heinemann Library, 2005
Langley, Andrew. *History in Art: Ancient Egypt*. Oxford: Raintree, 2005

GLOSSARY

alabaster translucent (slightly see-through) creamy-white stone

anonymous name unknown

architect someone who designs a building and makes sure that it is properly built. In ancient Greek the word means "master builder".

bronze brownish-gold metal made from a mixture of copper and tin. It is hard wearing and easy to work with.

cartouche oval ring enclosing the (hieroglyphic) name and title of a king

chisel metal tool with a shaped tip

composition way things are arranged in a picture, so that the finished layout does not look a jumble

embalming preserving from decay

geometric type of design using regular lines and shapes

granite hard grey stone

graphic design drawing, painting, and arranging words, usually for a magazine, television, or advertising

hieroglyphics form of picture writing. The word means "sacred carving" in ancient Greek.

illuminated manuscript decorated handwritten book or document

inscription word or words carved or marked on a monument or stone

lapis lazuli semi-precious blue stone

limestone grey or creamy-white rock that is fairly easy to work with

mallet wooden hammer used to hit the end of a chisel when carving

mason person who cuts, shapes, and builds with stone

mineral rock and stone, found in the ground

mural painting created on a wall

papyrus marsh plant and the paper made from it

proportion when something is in proportion it is of a correct, or pleasing, balance and size

pyramid building with triangular sides which rise up from a square base and meet together at one point

quarry place where stone is taken out of the ground

relief scene carved in stone or wood

sandstone rock made of sand, usually red, yellow, brown, grey, or white

scribe ancient writer and artist

scroll layer of papyrus, pressed together, and rolled up. Scrolls were often many metres long.

symbol simplified sign, shape, or object that represents something else

technique way of doing things

tempera painting using pigment mixed with egg

vegetable gum a glue-like substance from certain plants

INDEX

Numbers in plain type (24) refer to the text.

Numbers in bold type (**28**) refer to an illustration.